PAT CONWAY PRESENTS

VOLUME 4

# the *very best*
# IRISH SONGS

**50 songs**

# & BALLADS

## WORDS, MUSIC & GUITAR CHORDS

OLD FAVOURITES AND MODERN CLASSICS, MADE FAMOUS THROUGHOUT THE WORLD BY
MARY BLACK, CHRISTY MOORE, THE DUBLINERS, AND MANY OTHERS.

*includes*
The Fields of Athenry
The Isle of Innisfree
Ride On
Sonny's Dream
Nancy Spain

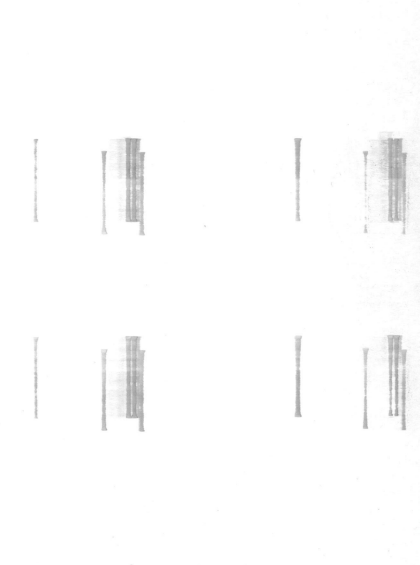

*Volume 4*

# CONTENTS

Bold Fenian Men, The ................................. 55

Bold O'Donoghue ....................................... 10

Bonny Boy, The ........................................... 61

Botany Bay .................................................. 57

Bould Thady Quill ....................................... 58

Boys from the County Armagh, The ..... 8

Crack Was Ninety, The ............................. 38

Danny Boy .................................................. 30

Down by the Glenside ............................... 21

Down by the Liffeyside ............................. 31

Fields of Athenry, The ............................... 15

Fiddlers Green ............................................ 5

German Clockwinder, The ........................ 43

Golden Jubilee, The ................................... 3

Green Fields of France, The ...................... 6

Henry My Son ............................................ 39

High Germany ............................................ 60

Highland Paddy .......................................... 45

Isle of Innisfree .......................................... 24

Kerry Recruit, The ..................................... 63

Lark in the Clear Air .................................. 53

Lark in the Morning, The .......................... 42

Look at the Coffin ..................................... 12

Love Thee Dearest ..................................... 16

Moonshiner, The ........................................ 47

My Lovely Rose of Clare ........................... 44

Nancy Spain ............................................... 26

Never Wed an Old Man ............................ 41

Ould Triangle, The ..................................... 46

Paddy Works on the Railway .................... 11

Patrick Was a Gentleman .......................... 34

Quare Bungle Rye ...................................... 54

Ride On ...................................................... 4

Rocky Road to Dublin, The ...................... 35

Rose of Allendale, The .............................. 22

Rosin the Bow ............................................ 51

Sally Brown ................................................ 37

Skibbereen .................................................. 64

Song for Ireland ......................................... 17

Sonny's Dream ........................................... 29

Spinning Wheel, The ................................. 48

Stone Outside Dan Murphy's Door, The.. 27

Sweet Carnlough Bay ................................ 18

Three Drunken Maidens ............................ 20

Three Score and Ten ................................. 19

Town of Ballybay, The .............................. 23

Twenty-One Years ..................................... 62

Weile Waile ................................................ 50

When You Were Sweet Sixteen ................. 2

Zoological Gardens, The ........................... 14

Copyright © 1999 Walton Manufacturing Ltd.

3-5 North Frederick Street, Dublin 1, Ireland

Produced by Pat Conway • Photos: The Irish Historical Picture Company

Design by Temple of Design • Printed in Ireland by Betaprint Ltd.

Order No. wm1322

ISBN No. 1 85720 095 0

*Exclusive Distributors:*

Walton Manufacturing Co. Ltd., Unit 6A, Rosemount Park Drive, Rosemount Business Park, Ballycoolin Road, Blanchardstown, Dublin 15, Ireland

Walton Music Inc., P.O. Box 874, New York, NY 10009, U.S.A.

1 3 5 7 9 0 8 6 4 2

# When You Were Sweet Sixteen

Written by James Thornton.

# The Golden Jubilee

Words & Music by Marie Doherty

*Arrangement copyright  Waltons Publications Ltd.*

Way down in the coun-ty Ker-ry in a place they call Tra-lee, A—
fine old cou-ple they lived there, named Kate and Pat Ma-gee. They were
go-ing to have a par-ty on their Gol-den Jub-i-lee, Now—
Kate says she to Pat Ma-gee, 'Come and lis-ten here to me.'size(10)

Chorus: (repeat after each verse)
Put on your ould knee breeches and your coat of emerald green.
Take off that hat, me darlin' Pat, put on your ould caubeen.
For today's our Golden Wedding and I'll have you all to know
Just how we looked when we were wed, fifty years ago.

Oh, well do I remember
How we danced on the village green.
You held me in your arms, dear Pat,
And called me your colleen.
Your hair was like a raven's wing,
But now it's turning grey.
Come over here oul' sweetheart dear,
And hear what I've to say.

And well do I remember
When first I was your bride,
In the little chapel on the hill
Where we stood side by side.
Of good friends we've had many,
Of troubles we've had few.
Come over here oul' sweetheart dear,
And here's what you must do.

*A Kerry Couple*

3

# Ride On

Written by one of Ireland's finest contemporary songwriters, Jimmy MacCarthy.

*Copyright Jimmy MacCarthy (MCPS)*

True you ride the fi - nest horse—— I've ev - er seen,——

Stand - ing six - teen one or two with

eyes wide and green. And you ride the

horse so well,—— hands light to the touch,

I could ne - ver go with you no mat - ter how I wan - ted to.

**Chorus**

Ride on, see you, I could ne - ver

go with you no mat - ter how I wan - ted to.

When you ride into the night without a trace behind,
Run your claw along my gut one last time.
I turn to face an empty space, where once you used to lie,
And look for a smile to light the night through a teardrop in my eye.
Chorus:-

# Fiddlers Green

This song, written by W. Connolly, was probably adapted from the 19th-century
sea shanty, 'Wrap Me Up in My Tarpaulin Jacket'.

*Copyright Hedley Music Group Ltd.*

As I walked by the dock-side one eve-ning so fair, To view the salt
wat-er and take the sea air, I heard an old fish-er-man sing-ing a song,
Won't you take me a - way boys, my time is not long. Wrap me
up in my oil-skin and jum-per, No more on the docks I'll be
seen. Just tell me oul' ship - mates I'm tak - ing a
trip mates, and I'll see you some day in Fid - dlers Green.

Now Fiddlers Green is a place I heard tell,
Where the fishermen go if they don't go to hell,
Where the skies are all clear and the dolphins do play
And the cold coast of Greenland is far, far away.
Chorus:-

When you get on the docks and the long trip is through,
There's pubs, there's clubs and there's lassies there too,
Where the girls are all pretty and the beer it is free,
And there's bottles of rum growing from every tree.
Chorus:-

Now, I don't want a harp nor a halo, not me,
Just give me a breeze and a good rolling sea.
I'll play me old squeeze-box as we sail along,
With the wind in the rigging to sing me a song.
Chorus:-

5

# The Green Fields of France

Like 'The Band Played Waltzing Matilda', this great anti-war song
was written by Scottish songwriter Eric Bogle.

Well how do you do, young Will-ie Mc - Bride? Do you mind if I

sit here down by your grave - side, And rest for a while 'neath the

warm sum - mer sun? I've been work - ing all day and__ I'm near - ly

done.__ I see by your grave - stone you were on - ly nine - teen When you

joined the great fall-en in nine-teen six - teen.__ I hope you died well, and I

hope you died clean. Or young Will - ie Mc - Bride was it slow and ob -

scene? Did they beat the drum slow - ly, did they play the fife

low - ly? Did they sound the dead march as they lo - wered you down?__

__ Did the band play the last post and cho - rus,__ Did the

pipes play the Flowers of the For - est?__

6

Did you leave e'er a wife or a sweetheart behind?
In some faithful heart is your memory enshrined?
Although you died back in nineteen sixteen,
In that faithful heart are you forever nineteen?
Or are you a stranger without even a name,
Enclosed in forever behind a glass frame,
In an old photograph torn, battered and stained
And faded to yellow in a brown leather frame?
Chorus:- (repeat after each verse)

The sun now it shines on the green fields of France,
There's a warm summer breeze makes the red poppies dance.
And see how the sun shines from under the clouds,
There's no gas or barbed wire, there's no guns firing now.
But here in this graveyard it's still no-man's land,
There's countless white crosses stand mute in the sand,
To man's blind indifference to his fellow man,
To a whole generation who were butchered and damned.

Young Willie McBride, I can't help wonder why,
Do all those that lie here know why did they die?
And did they believe, when they answered the call,
Did they really believe that this war would end wars?
The sorrow, the suffering, the glory, the pain,
The killing and dying was all done in vain,
For young Willie McBride it's all happened again,
And again and again and again and again.

*French Soldiers off to War, 1914*

# The Boys from the County Armagh

Traditional

*Copyright Waltons Publications Ltd.*

I've travelled that part of the County,
Through Newtown, Forkhill, Crossmaglen.
Around by the Gap of Mount Norris,
And home by Blackwater again.
Where girls are so gay and so hearty,
None fairer you'll find near or far,
But where are the boys that can court them,
Like the boys from the County Armagh?
Chorus:-

*Scotch Street, Armagh*

9

# Bold O'Donoghue

Traditional

*Arrangement copyright Waltons Publications Ltd.*

'Tis here I am from Pad-dy's land, a land of high re-nown.— I broke the hearts of
all the girls for miles from Kea-dy Town.— And when they hear that I'm a-wa' they'll
raise a hull-a-bal-oo,— When they hear a-bout the hand-some lad they call O' Don-ogh-
ue. **Chorus** For I'm the boy to please her and I'm the boy to
tease her, And I'm the boy to squeeze her and I'll tell you what I'll do.— I'll
court her like an I-rish-man with me brogue and blar-ney too is me plan, With me
roll-ik-in swoll-ik-in goll-ik-in woll-ik-in bold O' Don-ogh-ue.

I wish me love was a red, red rose growin' on yon garden wall,
And me to be a dew drop and upon her brow I'd fall.
Perhaps now she might think of me as a rather heavy dew,
No more she'd love the handsome lad they call O'Donoghue.
Chorus:-

They say that Queen Victoria has a daughter fine and grand,
Perhaps she'd take it into her head for marry an Irishman.
And if I could only get the chance to have a word or two,
Perhaps she'd take a notion in the bold O'Donoghue.
Chorus:-

# Paddy Works on the Railway

This ballad is also known as 'Paddy Works on the Erie', referring to the Erie Canal.
Many Irishmen also worked on the building of the American Transcontinental Railway.

*Arrangement copyright  Waltons Publications Ltd.*

In— eight-een hun-dred and for-ty one, my cor-du-roy breech-es I— put on, My— cor-du-roy bree-ches I put on to— work up-on the rail-way, The rail-way, I'm wea-ry of the rail-way, poor— Pad-dy works on the rail-way.

In eighteen hundred and forty-two, I didn't know what I should do,
I didn't know what I should do, to work upon the railway,
Chorus:-

In eighteen hundred and forty-three, I took a trip across the sea,
I took a trip across the sea, to work upon the railway,
Chorus:-

In eighteen hundred and forty-four, I landed on Columbia's shore,
I landed on Columbia's shore, to work upon the railway,
Chorus:-

In eighteen hundred and forty-five, when Daniel O'Connell was alive,
When Daniel O'Connell was alive, to work upon the railway,
Chorus:-

In eighteen hundred and forty-six, I changed my trade to carrying bricks,
I changed my trade to carrying bricks, to work upon the railway,
Chorus:-

In eighteen hundred and forty-seven, poor Paddy was thinking of going to heaven,
Poor Paddy was thinking of going to heaven, to work upon the railway,
Chorus:-

In eighteen hundred and forty-eight, I learnt to take my whiskey straight,
I learnt to take my whiskey straight, to work upon the railway,
Chorus:-

# Look at the Coffin

Also called 'Isn't It Grand Boys', this is an old English music hall song.

*Arrangement copyright  Waltons Publications Ltd.*

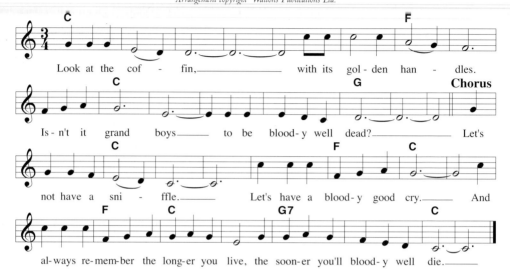

Look at the cof - fin,_____ with its gol - den han - dles.

Is - n't it grand boys___ to be blood- y well dead?_____ Let's

not have a sni - ffle._____ Let's have a blood- y good cry.___ And

al - ways re-mem-ber the long- er you live, the soon-er you'll blood- y well die._____

Look at the flowers all bloody withered. Isn't it grand boys to be bloody well dead?
Chorus:- (repeat after each verse)

Look at the mourners, bloody great hypocrites. Isn't it grand boys to be bloody well dead?

Look at the choir, bloody great tonsils. Isn't it grand boys to be bloody well dead?

Look at the preacher, bloody sanctimonious. Isn't it grand boys to be bloody well dead?

*Turning the Hay*

The Turf Carriers, Galway City

# The Zoological Gardens

This light-hearted song was written in the 19th century.
The Zoological Gardens are located in the Phoenix Park, Dublin.

*Arrangement copyright Walton Publications Ltd.*

Oh thun - der and light - ning it's— no lark, when Dub - lin
Ci - ty is in the dark. If you've an - y mon - ey go up to the
Park, and view the Zoo - log - ic - al Gar - dens.

Last Sunday night we had no dough, so I took the mot up to see the Zoo.
We saw the lions and the kangaroos, inside the Zoological Gardens.

We went out there by Castleknock. Said the mot to me, 'Sure we'll court by the Lough.'
And I knew she was one of the rare old stock, inside the Zoological Gardens.

Said the mot to me, 'My dear friend Jack would like a ride on the elephant's back.'
If you don't get out a that I'll give you such a crack, inside the Zoological Gardens.

We went out there on our honeymoon. Said the mot to me, 'If you don't come soon,
I'll have to sleep with the hairy baboon inside the Zoological Gardens.'

*A Jaunting Car, Phoenix Park, Dublin*

14

# The Fields of Athenry

This song, written by Dublin-born Pete St. John, has become a modern classic.

*Copyright Pete St. John (MCPS)*

By a lonely prison wall, I heard a young man calling,
'Nothing matters Mary when you're free.
Against the famine and the Crown, I rebelled, they shot me down.
Now you must raise our child with dignity.'
Chorus:-

By a lonely harbour wall, she watched the last star falling,
As that prison ship sailed out against the sky.
Sure she'll wait and hope and pray for her love in Botany Bay.
It's so lonely round the fields of Athenry.
Chorus:-

# Love Thee Dearest

Written by Thomas Moore (1779-1852).

*Arrangement copyright Waltons Publications Ltd.*

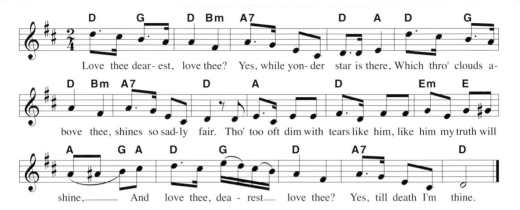

Love thee dear-est, love thee? Yes, while yon-der star is there, Which thro' clouds a-bove thee, shines so sad-ly fair. Tho' too oft dim with tears like him, like him my truth will shine,——— And love thee, dea - rest— love thee? Yes, till death I'm thine.

Love thee dearest, love thee? No, that star is not more true.
When my vows deceive thee, he will wander too.
A cloud of night may veil his light, and death shall darken mine.
But leave thee dearest, leave thee? No, till death I'm thine.

*Church Street, Athenry, Co. Galway*

16

# Song for Ireland

A love song for Ireland, written by Englishman Phil Colclough.

*Copyright Misty River Music*

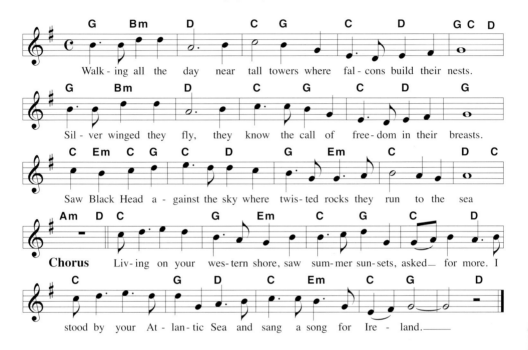

Walk - ing all the day near tall towers where fal - cons build their nests.

Sil - ver winged they fly, they know the call of free - dom in their breasts.

Saw Black Head a - gainst the sky where twis - ted rocks they run to the sea

**Chorus** Liv - ing on your wes - tern shore, saw sum - mer sun - sets, asked— for more. I

stood by your At - lan - tic Sea and sang a song for Ire - land.———

Talking all the day, with true friends who try to make you stay,
Telling jokes and news, singing songs to pass the night away.
Watched the Galway salmon run, like silver, dancing, darting in the sun.
Chorus:-

Drinking all the day, in old pubs where fiddlers love to play,
Saw one touch the bow, he played a reel which seemed so grand and gay.
Stood on Dingle beach and cast, in wild foam we found Atlantic bass.
Chorus:-

Dreaming in the night, I saw a land where no one has to fight.
Waking in your dawn, I heard you crying in the morning light.
Lying where the falcons fly, they twist and turn all in your rare blue sky.
Chorus:-

# Sweet Carnlough Bay

This song was written by McKay, a poet from Northern Ireland.
The air is that of a Scottish song, 'The Road to Dundee'.

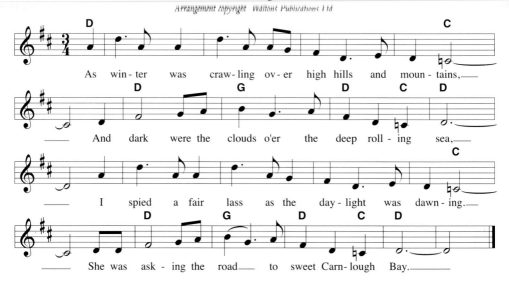

As win-ter was craw-ling ov-er high hills and moun-tains,—
—— And dark were the clouds o'er the deep roll-ing sea,—
—— I spied a fair lass as the day-light was dawn-ing.—
—— She was ask-ing the road— to sweet Carn-lough Bay.—

I said, 'My fair lass, I surely will tell you,
The road and the number of miles it will be,
And if you'll consent I'll convey you a wee bit,
And I'll show you the road to sweet Carnlough Bay.

You turn to the right and go down to the churchyard,
Cross over the river and down by the sea.
We'll stop at Pat Hamill's and have a wee drop there,
Just to help us along to sweet Carnlough Bay.

Here's a health to Pat Hamill, likewise the dear lassie,
And all you young laddies who're listening to me,
And ne'er turn your back on a bonnie young lassie,
When she's asking the road to sweet Carnlough Bay.'

# Three Score and Ten

## Traditional

*Arrangement copyright  Waltons Publications Ltd.*

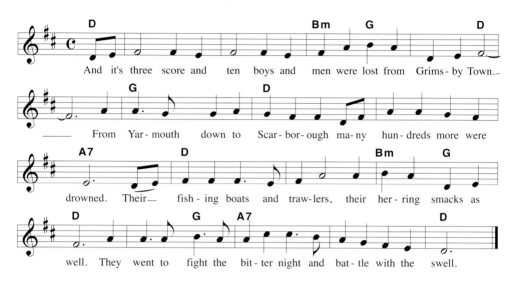

And it's three score and ten boys and men were lost from Grims-by Town.— From Yar-mouth down to Scar-bor-ough ma-ny hun-dreds more were drowned. Their— fish-ing boats and traw-lers, their her-ring smacks as well. They went to fight the bit-ter night and bat-tle with the swell.

Me thinks I see a host of craft spreading their sails a-lea,
As down the Humber they did lie, bound for the cold North sea.
Me thinks I see's a wee small craft, and crew with hearts so brave.
They want to earn their daily bread, upon the restless waves.

October night brought such a sight, 'twas never seen before.
There were masts and yards of broken spars washed-up on the shore.
There was many a heart of sorrow, there was many a heart so brave,
There was many a true and noble lad to find a watery grave.

*Harbour Road, Carnlough, Co. Antrim*

# Three Drunken Maidens

Traditional

*Arrangement copyright Waltons Publications Ltd.*

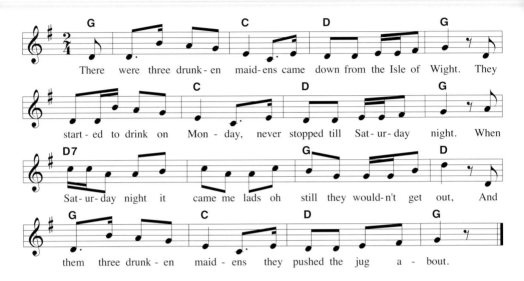

There were three drunk-en maid-ens came down from the Isle of Wight. They start-ed to drink on Mon-day, never stopped till Sat-ur-day night. When Sat-ur-day night it came me lads oh still they would-n't get out, And them three drunk-en maid-ens they pushed the jug a-bout.

Then in came dancing Sally, her cheeks a rosy bloom.
'Shove o'er you jolly sisters and give young Sal some room,
And I will be your equal before the evening's out.'
And them three drunken maidens, they pushed the jug about.

They had woodcock and pheasant, partridge and hare,
And every sort of dainty, no shortage there was there.
They'd forty pints of beer me lads but still they wouldn't get out,
And them three drunken maidens, they pushed the jug about.

Then in came the landlord, he was looking for his pay.
Forty pounds for beer me lads these girls were forced to pay.
They had ten pounds apiece me lads but still they wouldn't get out,
And them three drunken maidens, they pushed the jug about.

'Where are your fancy hats and your mantles rich and fine?'
'They've all been swallowed up me lads with tankards of fine wine.'
'And where are your fancy men, young maidens frisk and gay?'
'You left them in the ale house and it's there you'll have to pay.'

# Down by the Glenside

Another song written by Peadar Kearney, author of the Irish National Anthem.

*Copyright Waltons Publications Ltd.*

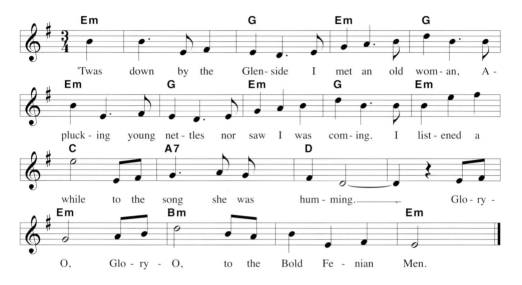

'Twas down by the Glen-side I met an old wom-an, A-pluck-ing young net-tles nor saw I was com-ing. I list-ened a while to the song she was hum-ming.——— Glo-ry-O, Glo-ry-O, to the Bold Fe-nian Men.

'Tis sixteen long years since I saw the moon beaming,
On brave manly forms and their eyes with heart gleaming.
I see them all now sure in all my day-dreaming,
Glory-O, Glory-O, to the bold Fenian Men.

Some died on the hillside, some died with a stranger,
And wise men have judged that their cause was a failure.
They fought for old Ireland and they never feared danger,
Glory-O, Glory-O, to the bold Fenian Men.

I passed on my way, thanks to God that I met her,
Be life long or short, sure I'll never forget her.
We may have brave men, but we'll never have better,
Glory-O, Glory-O, to the bold Fenian Men.

# The Rose of Allendale

This Scottish ballad has recently become popular in Ireland.

*Arrangement copyright Waltons Publications Ltd.*

Where'er I wandered, east or west, tho' fate began to lour,
A solace still she was to me, in sorrow's lonely hour.
When tempests lashed our lonely barque, and rent her shiv'ring sail,
One maiden form withstood the storm, 'twas the Rose of Allendale.
Sweet Rose of Allendale, sweet Rose of Allendale,
One maiden form withstood the storm, 'twas the Rose of Allendale.

And when my fever'd lips were parched on Afric's burning sands,
She whispered hopes of happiness, and tales of distant lands.
My life has been a wilderness, unblest by fortune's gale,
Had fate not linked my love to her, sweet Rose of Allendale.
Sweet Rose of Allendale, sweet Rose of Allendale,
Had fate not linked my love to her, sweet Rose of Allendale.

# The Town of Ballybay

Traditional

*Arrangement copyright Waltons Publications Ltd.*

In the town of Bal-ly-bay there is a lass-y dwell-ing. I knew her ve-ry well and the
sto-ry is worth tell-ing. Her fath-er kept a still and he was a good dist-ill-er.
When she took to drink well the dev-il would not fill her. With my ring-a-ding-a-dum and me
ring-a-ding-a-di-di-os, me ring-a-ding-a-dum whack fol-a-ding-da-di-os.

And she had a wooden leg that was hollow down the middle.
She used to tie a string on it and play it like a fiddle.
She fiddled in the hall, she fiddled in the alleyway,
She didn't give a damn, she had to fiddle anyway.
Chorus:- (Repeat after each verse)

And she said she couldn't dance unless she had her wellie on,
But when she had it on she could dance as well as anyone.
She wouldn't go to bed unless she had her shimmy on,
But when she had it on she would go as quick as anyone.

She had lovers by the score, every Tom and Dick and Harry.
She was courting night and day, but still she wouldn't marry.
And then she fell in love with a fella with a stammer.
When he tried to run away, she hit him with a hammer.

She had childer up the stairs, she had childer in the brier,
And another ten or twelve sitting roaring by the fire.
She fed them on potatoes and on soup she made with nettles,
And on lumps of hairy bacon that she boiled up in the kettle.

So she led a sheltered life eating porridge and black pudding,
And she terrorised her man until he died right sudden.
And when the husband died she was feeling very sorry.
She rolled him in a bag and she threw him in a quarry.

# Isle of Innisfree

Words & Music by Richard Farrelly

*Copyright Peter Maurice Music Co. Ltd. Reproduced by kind permission of IMP Ltd.*

I've met some folk who say that I'm a dream-er,____ And I've no
doubt there's truth in what they say.____ But sure a bo-dy's bound to be a
dream-er____ when all the things he loves are far a-way.____ And prec-ious
things are dreams un-to an ex-ile,____ They take him o'er the land a-cross the
sea,____ Es-pec-ially when it hap-pens he's an ex-ile,____ From that dear
love-ly Isle of In-nis-free.____ And when the moon-light peeps a-cross the
roof-tops____ of this great ci-ty, won-drous tho' it be____ I scarce-ly
feel its won-der or its laugh-ter____ I'm once a-gain back home in In-nis-free.____

I wander o'er green hills and dreamy valleys, and find a peace no other land could know,
I hear the birds make music fit for angels, and watch the rivers laughing as they flow.
And then into a humble shack I wander, my dear old home, and tenderly behold
The folk I love around the turf fire gather, on bended knees the rosary is told.
But dreams don't last though dreams are not forgotten, and soon I'm back to stern reality,
But though they pave the footpaths here with gold dust, I still would choose my Isle of Innisfree.

*Peasant Girl Gathering Seaweed*

# Nancy Spain

Written by the contemporary songwriter Barney Rushe.

*Copyright Rushe / Mild Music*

Of all the stars that ev-er shone not one does twin-kle like your pale blue eyes,

Like gold-en corn at har-vest time your hair._____ Sail-ing in my

boat the wind gent-ly blows and fills my sails, Your sweet scent-ed

breath is ev'-ry-where._____ No mat-ter where I wan-der I'm still

**Chorus**

haunt-ed by your name._____ The por-trait of your beau-ty stays the

same._____ Stand-ing by the o-cean wond'-ring where you've gone, if

you'll re-turn a-gain._____ Where is the ring I gave to Nan-cy Spain?_____

Daylight peeping through the curtains of the passing night time is your smile,
The sun in the sky is like your laugh.
Come back to me my Nancy, linger for just a little while,
Since you left these shores I know no peace nor joy.
Chorus:–

On the day in spring when the snow starts to melt and streams to flow,
With the birds I'll sing to you a song.
In the while I'll wander down by bluebell grove where wild flowers grow,
And I'll hope that lovely Nancy will return.
Chorus:-

# The Stone Outside Dan Murphy's Door

Johnny Patterson, a native of Ennis, Co. Clare who starred as a clown in
Barnum's circus, adapted 'The Rambler from Clare' as his signature tune.

There's a sweet gar-den spot in our mem'-ry,____ It's the place we were
born and reared.____ 'Tis long years a-go since we left it,____ But re-
turn there we will if we're spared.____ Our friends and com-pan-ions of childhood, would as-semb-le each night near a score,____ Round
Dan Murph-y's shop, and how of-ten we've sat On the stone that stood

**Chorus**

out-side his door!____ Those days in our hearts we will
cher-ish, Con-tent-ed al-though we were poor,____
____ And the songs that were sung in the days we were young, On the
stone out-side Dan Murph-y's door.____

27

When our day's work was over we'd meet there, in the winter or spring the same,
The boys and girls all together, then would join in some innocent game.
Dan Murphy would bring down his fiddle, while his daughters looked after the store,
The music would ring, and sweet songs we would sing, on the stone outside Dan
  Murphy's door.

Back again will our thoughts often wander, to the scenes of our childhood's home,
The friends and companions we left there, it was poverty caused us to roam.
Since then in this life we have prospered, but now still in our hearts we feel sure.
For mem'ry will fly to the days now gone by, and the stone outside Dam Murphy's door.

*Glengarriff and Killarney Coach Tour*

# Sonny's Dream

Written by Ron Hynes from Nova Scotia, Canada.

*Copyright Morning Music*

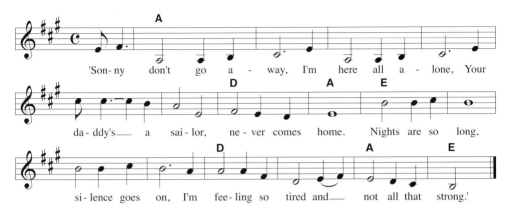

'Son-ny don't go a - way, I'm here all a - lone, Your da-ddy's— a sai-lor, ne-ver comes home. Nights are so long, si-lence goes on, I'm fee-ling so tired and— not all that strong.'

Sonny lives on a farm on a wide open space.
'Take off your shoes son, stay out of the race,
Lay down your head by the soft river bed.'
Sonny always remembers the words Mama said.

Sonny works on the land, though he's barely a man.
There's not much to do, he does just what he can.
He sits at the window of his room by the stairs,
He watches the waves gently wash on the pier.

Many years have gone by, Sonny's old and alone.
His Daddy the sailor never came home.
Sometime he wonders what his life might have been,
But from the grave Mama still haunts his dreams.

# Danny Boy

The air to this song was published in the George Petrie *Collection*. This, the most
popular version, was written by Fred F. Weatherly (1848-1929).

*Arrangement copyright Waltons Publications Ltd.*

And when ye come, and all the flowers are dying,
If I am dead, as dead I well may be,
You'll come and find the place where I am lying,
And kneel and say an Ave there for me.
And I shall hear, tho' soft you tread above me,
And all my grave will warmer, sweeter be,
If you will bend and tell me that you love me,
Then I shall sleep in peace until you come to me.

# Down by the Liffeyside

Peadar Kearney originally called this song, set to the air 'Down By the Slaney Side',
'Fish and Chips'. 'A one and one' is old Dublin slang for a serving of fish and chips.

*Copyright Waltons Publications Ltd.*

'Twas down by An-na Lif - fey my love and I did stray,___ Where-
in the good oul' slush-y mud___ the sea-gulls sport and play.___ We
got the whiff of ray and chips___ and Ma-ry soft-ly sighed,___ 'Ar-ah!
John won't you come for a one-and-one down___ by___ the___ Lif - fey-side?'___

Then up along by George's Street the loving pair did view,
And Mary swanked it like a queen in a skirt of navy-blue.
Her hat was lately turned and her blouse was newly dyed,
Sure you couldn't beat her amber locks, down by the Liffeyside.

And on her old melodion how sweetly she did play.
She played 'Goodbye' and 'Do Not Sigh' and 'Down by Texas Way'.
And when she turned Sinn Féiner, I nearly burst with pride,
For to hear her sing 'The Soldier's Song', down by the Liffeyside.

On Sunday morning to Meath Street, together we would go,
And up to Father Murphy where we both would take our vows.
He'll join our hands in wedlock bands and soon we'll be outside,
For a whole afternoon on our honeymoon, down by the Liffeyside.

And we'll have little children and rear them neat and clean,
To shout, 'Up the Republic' and to sing about Sinn Féin.
They'll do as their old fellows did, to England's power defy,
Send them off with guns against the Free-State huns, down by the Liffeyside.

*Topping the Turnips*

# Patrick Was a Gentleman

Traditional

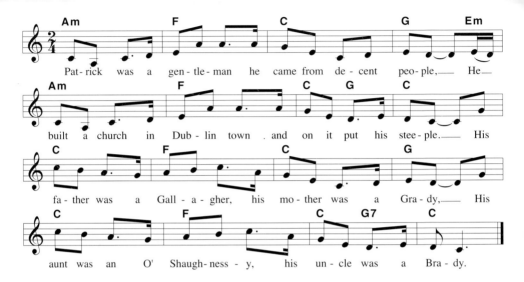

Pat-rick was a gen-tle-man he came from de-cent peo-ple,—— He—— built a church in Dub-lin town . and on it put his stee-ple.—— His fa-ther was a Gall-a-gher, his mo-ther was a Gra-dy,—— His aunt was an O' Shaugh-ness-y, his un-cle was a Bra-dy.

The Wicklow hills are very high, and so is the hill of Howth, sir,
But there's a hill much higher still, much higher than them both, sir.
On the top of this high hill St. Patrick preached his sermon,
Which drove the frogs into the bogs, and banished all the vermin.

There's not a mile of Erin's Isle where dirty vermin musters,
Where'ere he put his dear forefoot he murdered them in clusters.
The frogs went hop, the toads went plop, slapdash into the water,
And the beasts committed suicide to save themselves from slaughter.

Nine hundred thousand reptiles blue he charmed with sweet discourses,
And dined on them in Killaloo in soups and second courses.
Where blind worms crawling in the grass disgusted all the nation,
Right down to Hell with a holy spell he changed their situation.

No wonder that them Irish lads should be so gay and frisky,
Sure St. Pat he taught them that as well as making whiskey.
No wonder that the saint himself should understand distilling,
For his mother kept a shebeen shop in the town of Enniskillen.

Was I but so fortunate as to be back in Munster,
I'd be bound that from that ground I never more would once stir.
There St. Patrick planted turf, cabbages and praties,
Pigs galore, mo ghrá, mo stór, altar boys and ladies.

# The Rocky Road to Dublin

This song was probably written in the 19th century, set to a well-known slip jig.
It is a lively and popular ballad, sung to the rhythm of a slip jig.

*Arrangement copyright Waltons Publications Ltd.*

In Mullingar that night I rested limbs so weary,
Started by daylight next morning light and airy.
Took a drop of the pure, to keep my heart from sinking,
That's an Irishman's cure, when e'er he's on for drinking.
To see the lassies smile, laughing all the while,
At my curious style, 'twould set your heart a-bubbling.
They ax'd if I was hired, the wages I required,
'Till I was almost tired of the rocky road to Dublin.
Chorus:- (repeat after each verse)

In Dublin next arrived, I thought it such a pity,
To be so soon deprived a view of that fine city.
When I took a stroll among the quality,
My bundle it was stole in that neat locality.
Something crossed my mind, then I looked behind,
No bundle I could find upon my stick a-wobblin'.
Enquirin' for the rogue, they said my Connaught brogue,
Wasn't much in vogue on the rocky road to Dublin.

From there I got away, my spirits never failin',
Landed on the Quay as the ship was sailin'.
Captain at me roared, said that no room had he,
When I jumped aboard, a cabin found for Paddy.
Down among the pigs, I played some funny rigs,
Danced some hearty jigs, the water round me bubblin'.
When off to Holyhead I wished myself was dead,
Or better far instead, on the rocky road to Dublin.

The boys of Liverpool, when we safely landed,
Called myself the fool, I could no longer stand it.
Blood began to boil, temper I was losin',
Poor old Erin's Isle they began abusin'.
Hurrah me soul said I, me shillelagh I let fly,
Some Galway boys came by, they saw I was a hobblin'.
With a loud hurray, they joined in the affray,
And quickly cleared the way for the rocky road to Dublin.

*Sackville Street (now O'Connell Street), Dublin*

# Sally Brown

Traditional

*Arrangement copyright Waltons Publications Ltd.*

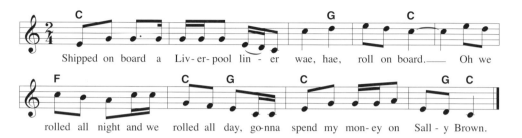

Shipped on board a Liv-er-pool lin - er wae, hae, roll on board.—— Oh we
rolled all night and we rolled all day, go-nna spend my mon-ey on Sall - y Brown.

Miss Sally Brown she's a nice young lady, way, hae, roll on board.
Oh we rolled all night and we rolled all day,
Gonna spend my money on Sally Brown.

Her mammy doesn't like a tarry sailor, way, hae, roll on board.
Oh we rolled all night and we rolled all day,
Gonna spend my money on Sally Brown.

She wants her to marry a one-legged Captain, wae, hae, roll on board.
Oh we rolled all night and we rolled all day,
Gonna spend my money on Sally Brown.

*Back from the Fair, Connemara*

# The Crack Was Ninety in the Isle of Man

Words & Music by Barney Rushe

*Copyright Rush / Mild Music*

Were-n't we the rare oul' stock, spent the eve-nin' get-tin' locked, In the Ace of

Hearts where the high stools were en-gag-ing. Ov-er the Butt Bridge, down by the dock,

the boat she sailed at five o'clock, Hu-rry boys, said Whack, or be-fore we're there we'll all be

back, Car-ry him if you— can, the— crack was nine-ty in the Isle of Man.

Before we reached the Alexander Base, the ding dong we did surely raise,
In the bar of the ship we had great sport, as the boat she sailed out of the port.
Landed up in the Douglas Head, enquired for a vacant bed,
The dining room we soon got shown by a decent woman up the road.
'Lads, ate it if you can,' the crack was ninety in the Isle of Man.

Next morning we went for a ramble round, viewed the sights of Douglas Town,
Then we went for a mighty session, in a pub they call Dick Darbies.
We must have been drunk by half-past three, to sober up we went swimmin' in the sea.
Back to the digs for the spruce up, and while waitin' for the fry,
We all drew up our plan, the crack was ninety in the Isle of Man.

That night we went to the Texas Bar, came back down by horse and car,
Met Big Jim and all went in to drink some wine in Yate's.
The Liverpool Judies it was said, were all to be found in the Douglas Head,
McShane was there in his suit and shirt, them foreign girls he was tryin' to flirt,
Saying, 'Here girls, I'm your man,' the crack was ninety in the Isle of Man.

Whacker fancied his good looks, on an Isle of Man woman he was struck,
But a Liverpool lad was by her side, and he throwin' the jar into her.
Whacker thought he'd take a chance, he asked the quare one out to dance,
Around the floor they stepped it out, and to Whack it was no bother.
Everythin' was goin' to plan, the crack was ninety in the Isle of Man.

The Isle of Man woman fancied Whack, your man stood there till his mates came back.
Whack! they all whacked into Whack, and Whack was Whacked out on his back.
The police force arrived as well, banjoed a couple of them as well,
Landed up in the Douglas jail, until the Dublin boat did sail,
Deported every man, the crack was ninety in the Isle of Man.

# Henry My Son

It is believed by many that the tragic hero in this ballad was Randolf, Earl of Leinster, who died in 1232.

*Arrangement copyright  Waltons Publications Ltd.*

Where have you been all day, Hen - ry my son? Where have you been all day my be-lov-ed one? A - way in the mead-ow a-way in the mead-ow Make my bed, I've a pain in my head, and I want to lie down.

And what did you have to eat, Henry my son?
What did you have to eat, my beloved one?
Poison beans, poison beans,
Make my bed, I've a pain in my head, and I want to lie down.

And what colour were them beans, Henry my son?
What colour were them beans, my beloved one?
Green and yellow, green and yellow,
Make my bed, I've a pain in my head, and I want to lie down.

And what will you leave your mother, Henry my son?
What will you leave your mother, my beloved one?
A woollen blanket, a woollen blanket,
Make my bed, I've a pain in my head, and I want to lie down.

And what will you leave your children, Henry my son?
And what will you leave your children, my beloved one?
The keys of heaven, the keys of heaven,
Make my bed, I've a pain in my head, and I want to lie down.

And what will you leave your sweetheart, Henry my son?
And what will you leave your sweetheart, my beloved one?
A rope to hang her, a rope to hang her,
Make my bed, I've a pain in my head, and I want to lie down.

*Peasant and Turf Stack*

# Never Wed an Old Man

Traditional

*Arrangement copyright Waltons Publications Ltd.*

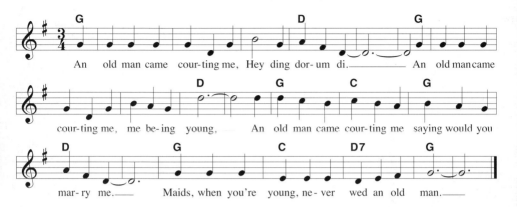

An old man came cour-ting me, Hey ding dor-um di._____ An old man came cour-ting me, me be-ing young, An old man came cour-ting me saying would you mar-ry me.___ Maids, when you're young, ne-ver wed an old man.___

Chorus:- (repeat after each verse)
Because he's got no falurum, fal-diddle-i-urum,
He's got no falurum fal-diddle-fal-day,
He's got no falurum, he's lost his ding durum.
Maids, when you're young, never wed an old man.

When we went to church, hey ding dorum di,
When we went to church, me being young,
When we went to church, he left me in the lurch.
Maids, when you're young, never wed an old man.

When we went to bed, hey ding dorum di,
When we went to bed, me being young,
When we went to bed, he lay like he was dead.
Maids, when you're young, never wed an old man.

When he lay fast asleep, hey ding dorum di,
When he lay fast asleep, me being young,
When he lay fast asleep, down the stairs I did creep,
Into the arms of a handsome young man.

# The Lark in the Morning

Traditional

*Arrangement copyright  Waltons Publications Ltd.*

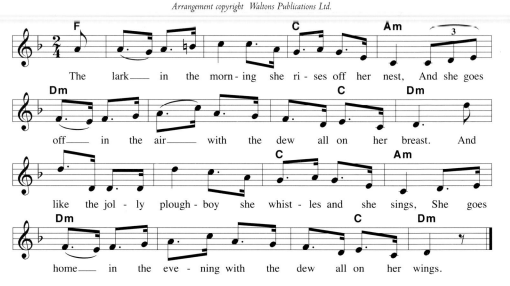

The lark— in the morn-ing she ri-ses off her nest, And she goes
off— in the air— with the dew all on her breast. And
like the jol-ly plough-boy she whist-les and she sings, She goes
home— in the eve-ning with the dew all on her wings.

Oh, Roger the ploughboy, he is a dashing blade,
He goes whistling and singing for yonder leafy shade.
He met with dark-eyed Susan, she's handsome I declare,
And she is far more enticing than the birds all in the air.

As they were coming home from the rakes of the town,
The meadow bein' all mown and the grass had been cut down.
As they should chance to tumble all on the new-mown hay,
'Oh, it's kiss me now or never,' this bonnie lass would say.

When twenty long weeks were over and past,
Her mammy asked the reason why she thickened round the waist.
'It was the pretty ploughboy,' this girl then did say,
'For he asked me for to tumble all on the new-mown hay.'

Here's a health to you ploughboys wherever you may be,
That like to have a bonnie lass a-sittin' on each knee.
With a pint of good strong porter he'll whistle and he'll sing,
And the ploughboy is as happy as a prince or a king.

# The German Clockwinder

Traditional

*Arrangement copyright Waltons Publications Ltd.*

A Ger-man clock-win-der to Dub-lin once came, Ben-ja-min Fooks was the old Ger-man's name. And as he was win-ding his way round the strand, He played on his flute and the mu-sic was grand. Sing-ing too ra-lom-a-lom-a, too-ra-lom-a-lom-a, too-ra-li ay, Too-ra-li you ra-li your a-li-ay, Too-ra loo-ma loo-ma, too ra loo-ma loom-a. toor a li-ay, Toor-a-li your a-li, your a-li-ay.

Oh there was a young lady from Grosvenor Square
Who said that her clock was in need of repair.
In walks the bould German and to her delight,
In less than five minutes he had her clock right.
Chorus:-

Now as they were seated down on the floor
There came this very loud knock on the door.
In walked her husband and great was his shock
For to see the ould German wind up his wife's clock.
Chorus:-

The husband says he, 'Now look here Mary Anne,
Don't let that bould German come in here again.
He wound up your clock and left mine on the shelf.
If your oul' clock needs winding, sure I'll wind it meself!'
Chorus:-

43

# My Lovely Rose of Clare

Words & Music by Chris Ball

*Copyright Asdee Music Co. Ltd.*

**Chorus**

Oh my love-ly Rose of Clare,— you're the sweet-est girl I know. You're the
queen of all the ro - ses like the pre-tty flowers that grow. You
are the sun-shine of my life, so beau-ti-ful and fair,——— For
I will al-ways love— you my lov-ely Rose of Clare.

The sun shone down just like a jewel on the lovely hills of Clare,
As I strolled along with my sweet lass, one evening at the fair.
Her eyes they shone like silver streams, her long and golden hair,
For I have won the heart of one, my lovely Rose of Clare.
Chorus:- (repeat after each verse)

We walked down by the river bank, watched the Shannon flowing by,
And listened to the nightingale singing songs for you and I.
And to say farewell to all you true and fair,
For I have stolen the heart of one, my lovely Rose of Clare.

# Highland Paddy

Traditional

*Arrangement copyright Waltons Publications Ltd.*

One even-ing fair as the sun was shin-ing,—— to Kil-ken-ny I did ride.
I did meet with Cap-tain Bra-dy,—— a tall com-man - der by his side.——

**Chorus**

—— Then you are wel - come High-land Pad-dy, by my side you'll sure-ly stand.
Hear the peo-ple shout for free-dom,—— we'll rise in the morn-ing with the
Fen - ian band, Rise in the morn-ing with the Fen - ian band.———.

In the mornin' we rose early, just before the break of dawn,
Blackbirds singing in the bushes, greetings to a smiling morn.
Gather 'round me, men of Ireland, gather Fenians gather round,
Hand to hand with sword and musket, spill the blood upon this holy ground.
Chorus:–

There's a glen beside the river, just outside Kilkenny Town.
There we met this noble captain, men lay dead upon the ground.
Chorus:–

There's a grave beside the river, a mile outside Kilkenny Town.
There we laid our noble captain, birds were silent when this Fenian died.
All my life I will remember, I'll remember night and day
That once I rode into Kilkenny, and I heard this noble captain say:
Chorus:–

# The Ould Triangle

Written by Brendan Behan for his play *The Quare Fellow*, set in Mountjoy Prison.
Dublin has two Canals: the Royal on the north side and the Grand on the south side.

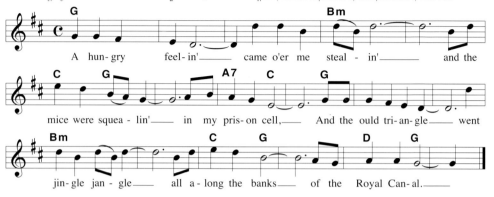

A hun- gry feel- in'_____ came o'er me steal - in'_____ and the
mice were squea - lin'_____ in my pris- on cell,_____ And the ould tri- an- gle_____ went
jin- gle jan - gle_____ all a - long the banks_____ of the Royal Can- al._____

To begin the morning, the warder's bawling, 'Get out of bed and clean up your cell.'
And that ould triangle went jingle jangle, all along the banks of the Royal Canal.

On a fine spring morning the lag lay dreaming, the seagulls wheeling high above the wall,
And that old triangle went jingle jangle, all along the banks of the Royal Canal.

The screw was peeping and the lag was sleeping, while he lay weeping for his girl Sal,
And that old triangle went jingle jangle, all along the banks of the Royal Canal.

The wind was rising and the day declining, as I lay pining in my prison cell,
And that old triangle went jingle jangle, all along the banks of the Royal Canal.

The day was dying and the wind was sighing, as I lay crying in my prison cell,
And that old triangle went jingle jangle, all along the banks of the Royal Canal.

In the female prison there are seventy women, I wish it was with them that I did dwell,
And that old triangle could go jingle jangle, all along the banks of the Royal Canal.

# The Moonshiner

Traditional

*Arrangement copyright  Waltons Publications Ltd.*

I've been a moon - shin- er for man - y a year, I've spent all my mon - ey on whisk - ey and beer. I'll go to some hol - low and set up my still, And I'll make you a gal - lon for a two dol - lar bill.

Chorus:-
I'm a rambler, I'm a gambler, I'm a long way from home,
If you don't like me, well leave me alone.
I'll eat when I'm hungry, I'll drink when I'm dry,
If moonshine won't kill me, I'll live till I die.

I'll go to some hollow in this counterie,
Ten gallons of wash I can go on the spree.
No woman to follow and the world is all mine,
I love none so well as I love the moonshine.
Chorus:—

Moonshine, dear moonshine, oh how I love thee,
You killed my poor father, but dare you try me.
Bless all moonshiners and bless all moonshine,
Its breath smells as sweet as the dew on the vine.
Chorus:—

I'll have moonshine for Liza and moonshine for May,
Moonshine for Lu and she'll sing all the day,
Moonshine for breakfast, moonshine for tea,
Moonshine, my hearties, it's moonshine for me.
Chorus:—

# The Spinning Wheel

This song was written by John Frances Waller, who was born in Limerick in 1809 of Tipperary parents and died in England in 1894. Deilia Murphy's version is the one most frequently sung.

Mel- low    the    moon-light    to    shine is    be - gin - ning,    Close by    the

win- dow    young Eil - een    is    spin - ning.    Bent o'er the    fire    her blind

grand- moth - er    sitt - ing    Is    croon-ing and    moan-ing    and    drows - i - ly

knitt- ing.    **Chorus**    Merr - i ly,    cheer - i ly,    noise-less-ly    whirr - ing    Swings the wheel,

spins    the wheel,    while the foot's    stirr - ing.    Sprite - ly and    light - ly    and

air - i - ly    ring- ing    Trills    the sweet    voice of the    young maid-en    sing - ing.

'Eileen, a chara, I hear someone tapping.'
"Tis the ivy dear mother against the glass flapping.'
'Eily, I surely hear somebody sighing.'
"Tis the sound mother dear of the autumn winds dying.'
Chorus:-

'What's the noise that I hear at the window I wonder?'
"Tis the little birds chirping, the holly-bush under.'
'What makes you be shoving and moving your stool on,
And singing all wrong the old song of 'The Coolin'?'
Chorus:-

There's a form at the casement, the form of her true love,
And he whispers with face bent, 'I'm waiting for you, love.
Get up from the stool, through the lattice step lightly,
And we'll rove in the grove while the moon's shining brightly.'

The maid shakes her head, on her lips lays her fingers,
Steps up from the stool, longs to go, and yet lingers.
A frightened glance turns to her drowsy grandmother,
Puts one foot on the stool, spins the wheel with the other.
Chorus:-

Lazily, easily, swings now the wheel round,
Slowly and lowly is heard now the reel's sound,
Noiseless and light to the lattice above her,
The maid steps then leaps to the arms of her lover.

Slower and slower and slower the wheel swings,
Lower and lower and lower the reel rings.
E're the reel and the wheel stop their ringing and moving,
Through the grove the young lovers by moonlight are roving.

*Spinning Wool*

# Weile Waile

Traditional

*Arrangement copyright Waltons Publications Ltd.*

There was an old wom- an and she lived in the woods, wei- le wei- le wai- le, There was an old wom-an and she lived in the woods, down by the riv- er Sái - le.

She had a baby three months old, weile weile waile,
She had a baby three months old, down by the river Sáile.

She had a pen-knife long and sharp, weile weile waile,
She had a pen-knife long and sharp, down by the river Sáile.

She stuck the pen-knife in the baby's heart, weile weile waile,
She stuck the pen-knife in the baby's heart, down by the river Sáile.

Three loud knocks came knocking on the door, weile weile waile,
Three loud knocks came knocking at the door, down by the river Sáile.

Two policemen and a dog, weile weile waile,
Two policemen and a dog, down by the river Sáile.

They took her away, and threw her into jail, weile weile waile,
They took her away, and threw her into jail, down by the river Sáile.

They put a rope around her neck, weile weile waile,
They put a rope around her neck, down by the river Sáile.

They pulled the rope and she got hung, weile weile waile,
They pulled the rope and she got hung, down by the river Sáile.

And that was the end of the woman in the woods, weile weile waile,
And that was the end of the baby too, down by the river Sáile.

And the moral of the story is, weile weile waile,
Don't stick knives in the baby's heart, down by the river Sáile.

# Rosin the Bow

Traditional
*Arrangement copyright Waltons Publications Ltd.*

I've trav-elled this world—— all o-ver,———— and now to a-noth-er I go,———— And I know that good quar-ters are wait-ing—— for to wel-come old Ro-sin the Bow.———— To wel-come old Ros-in the Bow me lad, to wel-come old Ros-in the Bow.———— And I know that good quart-ers are wait-ing—— for to wel-come old Ros-in the Bow.

When I'm dead and laid out on the counter, a voice you will hear from below,
Saying, 'Send down a hogshead of whiskey, to drink with old Rosin the Bow,
To drink with old Rosin the Bow, me lad, to drink with old Rosin the Bow.'
Saying, 'Send down a hogshead of whiskey, to drink with old Rosin the Bow.'

And get a half dozen stout fellows, and stack them all up in a row.
Let them drink out of half-gallon bottles, to the memory of Rosin the Bow,
To the memory of Rosin the Bow, me lad, to the memory of Rosin the Bow.
Let them drink out of half gallon bottles, to the memory of Rosin the Bow.

Get this half dozen stout fellows, and let them all stagger and go,
And dig a great hole in the meadow, and in it put Rosin the Bow,
And in it put Rosin the Bow, me lad, and in it put Rosin the Bow.
And dig a great hole in the meadow, and in it put Rosin the Bow.

Get ye a couple of bottles, put one at me head and me toe.
With a diamond ring scratch upon them, the name of old Rosin the Bow,
The name of old Rosin the Bow, me lad, the name of old Rosin the Bow
With a diamond ring scratch upon them, the name of old Rosin the Bow.

I feel that old tyrant approaching, that cruel remorseless old foe,
And I lift up me glass in his honour, take a drink with old Rosin the Bow,
Take a drink with old Rosin the Bow, me lad, take a drink with old Rosin the Bow.
And I lift up me glass in his honour, take a drink with old Rosin with Bow.

# Lark in the Clear Air

The lyrics to this song were written by Sir Samuel Ferguson (1810-1878).
The air is that of 'An Táilliúr' ('The Tailor').

*Arrangement copyright Waltons Publications Ltd.*

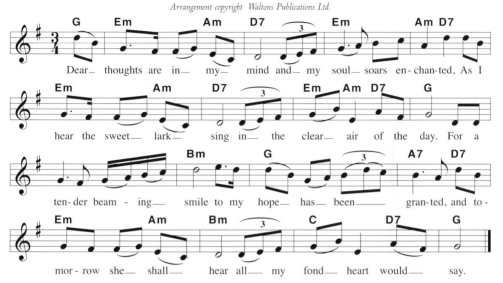

Dear— thoughts are in— my— mind and— my soul— soars en-chan-ted, As I hear the sweet— lark— sing in— the clear— air of the day. For a ten-der beam - ing— smile to my hope— has— been—— gran-ted, and to-mor-row she— shall— hear all— my fond— heart would— say.

I shall tell her all my love, all my soul's adoration,
And I think she will hear me, and will not say me nay.
It is this that gives my soul all its joyous elation,
As I hear the sweet lark sing in the clear air of the day.

*Glynn Village, Larne, Co. Antrim*

# Quare Bungle Rye

Traditional

*Arrangement copyright Waltons Publications Ltd.*

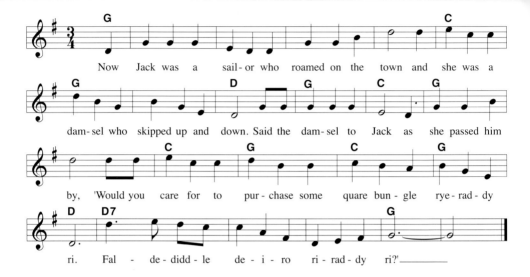

Now Jack was a sail-or who roamed on the town and she was a
dam-sel who skipped up and down. Said the dam-sel to Jack as she passed him
by, 'Would you care for to pur-chase some quare bun-gle rye-rad-dy
ri. Fal – de-didd-le de-i-ro ri-rad-dy ri?'_____

Thought Jack to himself, 'Now what can this be,
But the finest old whiskey from far Germany,
Smuggled up in a basket and sold on the sly,
And the name that it goes by is quare bungle rye,' etc.

Jack gave her a pound and he thought nothing strange.
She said, 'Hold on to the basket till I run for your change.'
Jack looked in the basket and a child he did spy.
'Begorrah' says Jack, 'this is quare bungle rye,' etc.

Now to get the child christened was Jack's next intent,
For to get the child christened, to the parson he went.
Said the parson to Jack, 'What will he go by?'
'Bedad now,' says Jack, 'call him Quare Bungle Rye,' etc.

Says the parson to Jack, 'There's a very queer name.'
'Bedad' now says Jack, ''twas the queer way he came.
Smuggled up in a basket and sold on the sly,
And the name that he'll go by is Quare Bungle Rye,' etc.

Now all you bold sailors who roam on the town,
Beware of the damsels who slipped up and down.
Take a peep in their baskets as they pass you by,
Or else they may pawn on you some quare bungle rye, etc.

# The Bold Fenian Men

This ballad was probably written by William Rooney around 1900. The Fenian Society
constituted a determined body of men who engineered the Risings of 1798, 1803 and 1848.

*Arrangement copyright  Waltons Publications Ltd.*

See who comes o - ver the red - bloss- omed heath- er, Their green ban - ners
kiss - ing the pure moun- tain air. Heads er - ect, eyes front, step - ping
proud - ly to - ge- ther, Sure free - dom sits throned on each proud spir - it
there. And down the hill twin- ing, their bless- ed steel shin- ing, Like ri- vers of
beau - ty that flow from each glen. From moun - tain and val - ley 'tis
li - ber- ty's ral- ly. Out and make way for the Bold Fen- ian Men.

Our prayers and our tears they have scoffed and derided,
They've shut out God's sunlight from spirit and mind.
Our foes were united and we were divided,
We met and they scattered our ranks to the wind.
But once more returning, within our veins burning,
The fires that illumined dark Aherlow Glen.
We raise the old cry anew, slogan of Conn and Hugh,
Out and make way for the bold Fenian Men!

We've men from the Nore, the Suir and the Shannon,
Let the tyrants come forth, we'll bring force against force.
Our pen is the sword and our voice is the cannon
Rifle for rifle and horse against horse.
We've made the false Saxon yield many a red battlefield,
God on our side, we will triumph again.
Pay them back woe for woe, give them back blow for blow,
Out and make way for the bold Fenian Men!

Side by side for the cause, have our forefathers battled,
When our hills never echoed the tread of a slave.
In many a field where the leaden hail rattled,
Through the red gap of glory, they marched to the grave.
And those who inherit their name and their spirit,
Will march 'neath the banner of Liberty then.
All who love foreign law, native or Sasanach,
Must out and make way for the bold Fenian Men!

*Market Cross, Killarney, Co. Kerry*

# Botany Bay

Traditional

*Arrangement copyright Waltons Publications Ltd.*

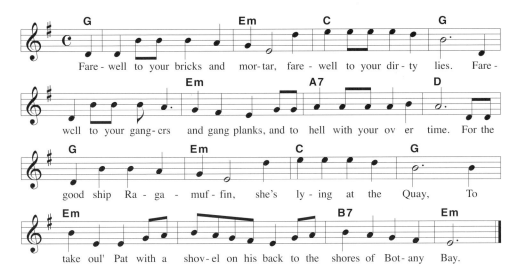

Fare - well to your bricks and mor-tar, fare - well to your dir-ty lies. Fare -
well to your gang-ers and gang planks, and to hell with your ov er time. For the
good ship Ra - ga - muf - fin, she's ly - ing at the Quay, To
take oul' Pat with a shov-el on his back to the shores of Bot-any Bay.

I'm on my way down to the quay where the ship at anchor lays,
To command a gang of navvys that they told me to engage.
I thought I'd drop in for a drink, before I went away,
For to take a trip on an emigrant ship, to the shores of Botany Bay.
Repeat first verse:-

The boss came up this morning, he says, 'Well Pat you know,
If you don't get your navvys out I'm afraid you'll have to go.'
So I asked him for my wages and demanded all my pay,
For I told him straight, 'I'm going to emigrate to the shores of Botany Bay.'
Repeat first verse:-

And when I reach Australia, I'll go and look for gold,
There's plenty there for the digging of, or so I have been told.
Or else I'll go back to my trade and a hundred bricks I'll lay,
Because I live for an eight hour shift on the shores of Botany Bay.
Repeat first verse:-

# Bould Thady Quill

This famous Cork ballad was written by Johnny Pat Gleeson.

*Arrangement copyright Waltons Publications Ltd.*

At the great hurling match between Cork and Tipperary,
'Twas played in the Park, on the banks of the Lee,
Our own darling boys were afraid of being beaten,
So they sent for bould Thady to Ballinagree.
He hurled the ball right and left in their faces
And showed the Tipperary boys action and skill.
If they touched on our lines he did manfully brave them,
And they put in the paper the praise of Thady Quill.
Chorus:-

Our Thady is famous in a great many places.
At the athletic races held down in Cloughroe,
He won the long jump without throwing off his waistcoat,
Going twenty-four feet from the heel to the toe.
And at throwing the weight, with Dublinman foremost,
Our own darling Thady exceeded him still.
And all 'round the field went the loud swinging chorus:
Long life and success to the bould Thady Quill.
Chorus:-

At the Cork Exhibition there was a fair lady,
Her fortune exceeded a million or more.
But a bad constitution had ruined her completely
And medical treatment had failed o'er and o'er.
'Yerrah, mamma,' says she, 'sure I know what will heal me
And cure the disease that is certain to kill.
Give over your doctors and medical treatment,
Let me have a stroll out with bould Thady Quill.'
Chorus:-

*Poitín Still*

# High Germany

Traditional

*Arrangement copyright Waltons Publications Ltd.*

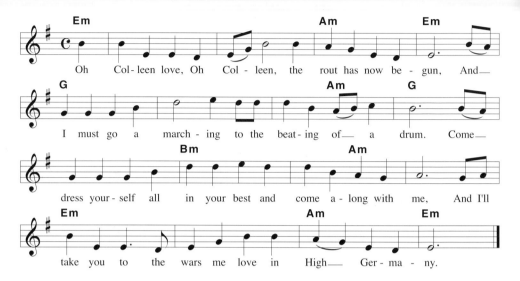

Oh Col-leen love, Oh Col-leen, the rout has now be-gun, And—
I must go a march-ing to the beat-ing of— a drum. Come—
dress your-self all in your best and come a-long with me, And I'll
take you to the wars me love in High— Ger-ma-ny.

I'll buy for you a horse me love, and on it you will ride,
And all of my delight will be in riding by your side.
We'll stop at every ale-house, and drink when we are dry,
We'll be true to one another and get married by and by.

O cursed be those cruel wars that ever they did rise,
And out of merry England pass many a man likewise.
They took my true-love from me, likewise my brothers three,
And sent them to the wars me love in high Germany.

My friends I do not value, and my foes I do not fear,
For now my fine love's left me, and wanders far and near.
And when my baby it is born, and smiling on my knee,
I'll think of handsome Willie in high Germany.

# The Bonny Boy

Of Scottish origin, this song tells the story of a girl of 21, married at the instigation
of her father to a boy of 16 who dies after the first year of marriage.

*Arrangement copyright  Waltons Publications Ltd.*

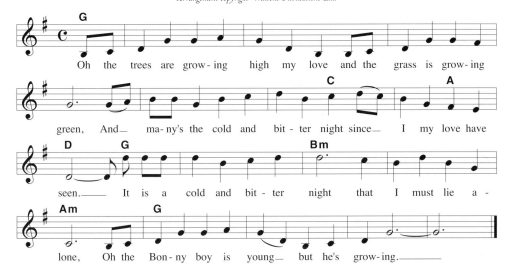

Oh father, dear father, I think you did me wrong,
For to go and get me married to one who is so young.
For he is but sixteen and I am twenty-one,
But the bonny boy is young but he's growing.

Oh daughter, dear daughter, I did not do you wrong,
For to go and get you married to one who is so young.
He will be a match for you when I am dead and gone,
Oh the bonny boy is young but he's growing.

Oh father, dear father, I'll tell you what I'll do,
I'll send my love to college for another year or two.
And all around his college cap I'll bind a ribbon blue,
To show the other girls that he's married.

'Twas at the age of sixteen years he was a married man,
And at the age of seventeen, the father of a son.
But at the age of eighteen, o'er his grave the grass grew high,
Cruel death put an end to his growing.

I will buy my love a shroud of the finest Holland Brown,
And whilst I am a-weaving it the tears they will flow down.
For once I had a true love but now he's lying low,
And I'll nurse his bonny boy while he's growing.

# Twenty-One Years

Traditional

*Arrangement copyright Waltons Publications Ltd*

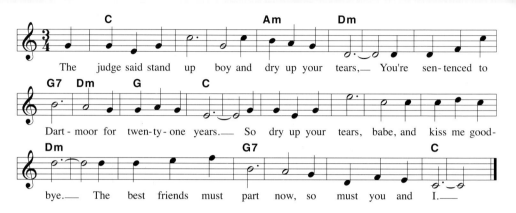

The judge said stand up boy and dry up your tears,— You're sen-tenced to Dart-moor for twen-ty-one years.— So dry up your tears, babe, and kiss me good-bye.— The best friends must part now, so must you and I.—

I hear the train coming, 'twill be here at nine,
To take me to Dartmoor to serve up my time.
I look down the railway, and plainly I see
You standing there waving your goodbyes to me.

Six months have gone by, babe, I wish I were dead.
This cold dreary dungeon and stone for my head.
It's raining, it's hailing, the moon shows no light.
Now will you tell me, babe, why you never write?

I've counted the days, babe, I've counted the nights,
I've counted the footsteps, I've counted the lights,
I've counted the raindrops, I've counted the stars,
I've counted a million of these prison bars.

I've waited, I've trusted, I've longed for one day,
A life-time so lonely, now my hair's turning grey.
And my thoughts are for you, babe, till I'm out of my mind,
For twenty-one years is a mighty long time,
For twenty-one years is a mighty long time.

# The Kerry Recruit

This anti-recruiting song is similar to 'The Recruiting Sergeant', written by Séamus O'Farrell in 1915.
Anyone heard singing this or other anti-recruiting songs was liable to six months' imprisonment.

*Arrangement copyright Waltons Publications Ltd.*

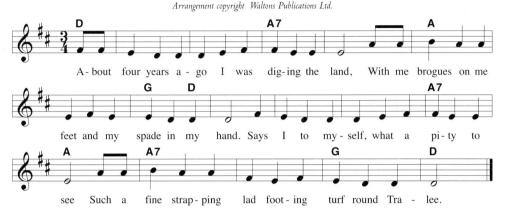

A-bout four years a-go I was dig-ing the land, With me brogues on me feet and my spade in my hand. Says I to my-self, what a pi-ty to see Such a fine strap-ping lad foot-ing turf round Tra - lee.

So I buttoned my brogues and shook hands with my spade,
And I went to the fair like a dashing young blade.
When up comes a sergeant and asks me to 'list.
'Arra, Sergeant, a grá, put the bob in my fist.'

And the first thing they gave me it was a red coat,
With a wide strap of leather to tie round my throat.
They gave me a quare thing, I asked what was that,
And they told me it was a cockade for my hat.

The next thing they gave me, they called it a gun,
With powder and shot and a place for my thumb.
And first she spit fire and then she spit smoke,
Lord, she gave a great lep and my shoulder near broke.

The next place they sent me was down to the sea,
On board of a warship bound for the Crimea.
Three sticks in the middle all rowled round with sheets,
Faith, she walked thro' the water without any feet.

We fought at the Alma, likewise Inkermann,
But the Russians they whaled us at the Redan.
In scaling the walls there myself lost my eye,
And a big Russian bullet ran off with my thigh.

It was there I lay bleeding, stretched on the cold ground,
Heads, legs and arms were scattered all around.
Says I, if my man or my cleaveens were nigh,
They'd bury me decent and raise a loud cry.

They brought me the doctor, who soon staunched my blood,
And he gave me an elegant leg made of wood.
They gave me a medal and tenpence a day,
Contented with Sheila, I'll live on half-pay.

# Skibbereen

This ballad was written after the Irish Famine, when many people were forced by
starvation, due to blight in the potato crop, to emigrate to the U.S.A.

*Arrangement copyright Waltons Publications Ltd.*

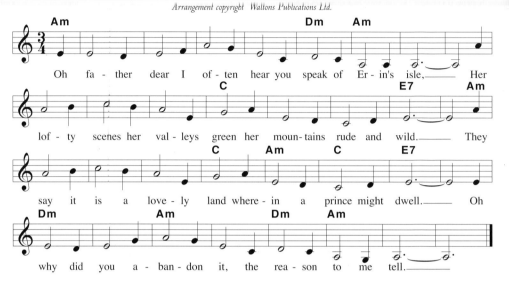

Oh father dear I often hear you speak of Er-in's isle, Her
lofty scenes her valleys green her mountains rude and wild. They
say it is a lovely land where-in a prince might dwell. Oh
why did you a-ban-don it, the rea-son to me tell.

Oh, son I loved my native land with energy and pride,
Till a blight came o'er my crops, my sheep, my cattle died.
My rent and taxes were too high, I could not them redeem,
And that's the cruel reason that I left old Skibbereen.

Oh, well do I remember the bleak December day,
The landlord and the sheriff came to drive us all away.
They set my roof on fire with cursed English spleen,
And that's another reason that I left old Skibbereen.

Your mother, too, God rest her soul, fell on the snowy ground,
She fainted in her anguish, seeing the desolation round.
She never rose, but passed away from life to mortal dream,
And found a quiet grave, my boy, in dear old Skibbereen.

And you were only two years old and feeble was your frame,
I could not leave you with my friends, you bore your father's name.
I wrapped you in my cotamore at the dead of night unseen,
I heaved a sigh and bade good-bye, to dear old Skibbereen.

Oh father dear, the day may come when in answer to the call,
Each Irishman, with feeling stern, will rally one and all.
I'll be the man to lead the van beneath the flag of green,
When loud and high we'll raise the cry – 'Remember Skibbereen'.